The Clueless Tourist's

PARIS TRAVEL GUIDE

The Clueless Tourist's

DISCLAIMER

CLUELESS TOURIST GUIDES

Clueless Tourist Guides are designed for people who want quick, easy, information about the destination they are visiting. Optimised for smartphones and tablets, as well as print editions, Clueless Tourist Guides are a must-have companion for your trip abroad, wherever in the world you are going!

Visit http://www.clueless-tourist.com for more information.

The Clueless Tourist's

CONTENTS

The Clueless Tourist's

The Clueless Tourist's

Paris - A Brief History

View over Paris, overlooking the Trocadero[i]

If there is one city in the world guaranteed to make the hairs on your arm stand up when you first see it then it is Paris. The marvellous French capital has long been viewed as being arguably the most picturesque, romantic, artistic, fashionable and downright interesting city on the planet.

With a long and fascinating history behind it, Paris has somehow managed to remain relevant and contemporary throughout centuries of change and progress that have occurred both in it and around it.

The Clueless Tourist's

The city dates all the way back to the 3rd century BC, when it was founded by a Celtic tribe. The excellent location of Paris made it an important trading centre and by the time the 12th century came along it was classed as being the biggest and most prosperous city in the western hemisphere.

During the following centuries the city was the scene of such historic developments as the setting up of one of Europe's first universities, a couple of massive international fairs and the world's first manned hot air balloon flight. Of course, it has also seen more than its fair share of war and protests too, along with the French Revolution, which started here and went on to shake the country and the rest of the world.

Paris Travel Guide

Paris in the 1890s

Throughout the history of Paris it has been regarded as a centre of art, fashion, cuisine, science and culture. It is also the home of cinema, as it is where the Lumière brothers first brought motion pictures to the screen for paying customers. The long and distinguished list of ex-residents of the city includes the likes of Pablo Picasso, Frederic Chopin, Marcel Proust, Vincent van Gogh, Jules Verne, Franz Liszt and many other famous people who were drawn to the City of Light.

The Clueless Tourist's

The immense popularity of Paris throughout the ages can be clearly seen by its strong presence in pop culture reference. The song "I Love Paris" is probably the most famous English language song about the French capital but it is far from the only one. The Eiffel Tower has also appeared in numerous films and it is common in comedies, dramas and romantic shows for the characters to make a short trip to this wonderful city. Famous films set here include An American in Paris, Last Tango in Paris and the classic Hunchback of Notre Dame.

With such a wealth of history and culture it is no surprise to discover that Paris has some of the most interesting museums, art galleries and cultural attractions to be seen anywhere in the world. The massive Louvre is the planet's most visited museum and is home to the Mona Lisa and the Venus de Milo statue, among many other pieces. In addition, the Musée National d'Art Moderne and the Musée d'Orsay are among the other museums here with richly captivating collections from throughout the centuries.

A simple stroll through Paris is enough to sense the rich history of the place. The Eiffel Tower, the Arc de Triomphe, the Moulin Rouge, Notre Dame and other iconic landmarks are all highly evocative and immediately make the city appear familiar to even the first time visitor.

By delving deeper into this magnificent travel destination it is possible to discover incredibly trendy zones, cosmopolitan areas with a strong ethnic mix and sprawling parks where picnics and cycling are common weekend pursuits.

Everyone who spends time in Paris looks for something different from it. Some want the famously romantic atmosphere to add a spark to their relationship while others want to enjoy world class shopping, to be inspired by art or to soak up the history of the place. No matter what reasons you have for visiting the French capital it makes sense to find out all about it and be prepared for a unique experience that you are unlikely to ever forget.

The Clueless Tourist's

Paris in Literature, Art, Music, Film

Rue Montorgueil, Claude Monet

The position of Paris at the forefront of world culture is made clear with simple look at a few of treasures that its incredible legacy has gifted us. Some of the most popular writers, artists, singers and film-makers of all time have either lived here or else used the city as inspiration for their creativity.

The Role of Paris in World Literature

Book-lovers will find the city of their dreams when they first set foot in Paris. The French capital has hundreds of diverse book stores, selling literature in English and other languages as well as in French. These stores range from tiny, cramped little spaces filled with rare second hand books to big international chains and historic, enormously atmospheric shops.

It was back in the mid-18th century that the first book was printed here. In the time that has passed since then Paris has remained as the heart of the French literary world. Most of the French publishing houses are located on the Left Bank, typically in the 5th, 6th and 7th arrondissements. This is also the area where lots of book stores and stalls can be found. Browsing books is a wonderful pastime here and something that many locals seem to get a lot of pleasure from too.

Interestingly, the importance of literature in France is such that writers and publishers are protected from books being too heavily discounted. However, the vast range of second hand tomes on sale means that there are always bargains to be picked up here.

Books Set in Paris

With Paris being such an exhilarating and diverse city, it is no surprise to find that many terrific books have been set here (as well as some pretty bad ones, to be fair).

Among the most well-known books in which all or part of the action takes place here are *The Hunchback of Notre Dame* by Victor Hugo, *A Tale of Two Cities* by Charles Dickens, *The Day of the Jackal* by Fredrick Forsyth, *The Da Vinci Code* by Dan Brown and *Interview with the Vampire* by Anne Rice.

Many of the best books set here use the city's unmistakeable landmarks to add to the story and the drama, presumably because we are all so familiar with them that we can easily imagine someone climbing up the Eiffel Tower or standing under the Arc De Triomphe.

A few of the famous French books set here that have never became quite so popular in English are *Le Père Goriot* by Honoré de Balzac, *Au Bonheur des Dames* by Émile Zola and *Gigi* by Colette. Anyone who understands the French language well enough to read a book in it will discover a world of literary magic both set in Paris and inspired by it.

The Clueless Tourist's

Famous Writers Who Lived in Paris

Statue of Alexandre Dumas, Place du Général Catroux à Paris XVIIème

The allure of Paris has traditionally been strong for
writers looking to find inspiration while living in a
great city. While the clichéd image is of a struggling

writer living a bohemian, decadent lifestyle here, it has also been home to many of history's finest and most successful authors too.

The list of French writers who lived here includes such giants of French literature as Alexandre Dumas, Voltaire, Colette, Marcel Proust, Victor Hugo and Jules Verne.

Among the foreign writers who have been attracted to live here or spend time here are Ernest Hemingway, Samuel Beckett, F.Scott Fitzgerald, Henry Miller, Oscar Wilde and Milan Kundera.

Art

The immense collection of treasures in the city's museums means that Paris has one of the richest and most comprehensive selections of art anywhere in the world. From classic pieces of art that everyone is aware of to cutting edge modern paintings and controversial sculptures, you will find them all here.

Art Galleries in Paris

Serious art fans may not be happy simply seeing the thousands of amazing items on display in the various museums here. In that case, a trip to a few of the city's art galleries could be a fine choice of activity.

There are many independent galleries here, selling and displaying all sorts of items. Modus Art Gallery, Galeria Xippas and La Maison Rouge are all well worth keeping an eye out for. Anyone who loves good art certainly won't be short of things to do and see, with enough museums and galleries to keep them busy for as long as they want.

Famous Artists Who Have Lived Here

The reputation of Paris as a city with a great art scene has led to some of the most famous artists of all time being drawn here to live and work. As well as the French born painters and sculptors who travelled to the capital, a number of the top international artists also set up home in Paris over the years.

This has led to the city being associated with the likes of Vincent van Gogh, Pablo Picasso, Paul Cézanne, Henri Rousseau and Henry Mattise over the centuries. In the present day, it is still an attractive city for artists and has a vibrant art scene in areas such as Le Marais, the Latin Quarter and République.

Famous Works of Art in Paris

'Mona Lisa' by Leonardo di Vinci

The Clueless Tourist's

The number of incredible museums and art galleries in Paris means that the city is stocked with one of the finest art collections in the world. It would be impossible to see even a fraction of the art on display here on a short trip, meaning that it is vital to work out which places hold the pieces that are most of interest to you.

World famous paintings such as the Mona Lisa, Liberty Leading the People, The Coronation of Napoleon, van Gogh's self-portraits and Virgin on the Rocks are among the invaluable treasures stored across the city in different locations.

There are also plenty of amazing sculptures spread across all of Paris too. Venus de Milo, The Thinker, the Winged Victory of Samothrace and the giant bronze statue of Louis XIV are among the most eye-catching sculptures in Paris.

Music

Parisian street musician[ii]

Paris is a city that has a wonderful musical background. The strong musical tradition here is also matched by the way in which the charms of Paris have encouraged many songwriters to wax lyrical about it over the decades.

Paris is famous for its music halls, for classic music, for jazz and for just about every other style around. In modern times it has gained a strong reputation for its exciting hip hop scene too.

Musicians Who Have Lived Here

Edith Piaf[iii]

The list of musicians who were born here or come to live here is hugely impressive and covers many different styles. Edith Piaf, Charles Aznavour, Jim Morrison, Serge Gainsbourg, Django Reinhardt, Maurice Chevalier, and Frederic Chopin are among those who have lived in this most musical and inspiring of cities.

Songs About Paris

The eternal charm of Paris has ensured that there is no shortage of songs about the city in different languages. In English the best known is probably "I

Love Paris", which was written by Cole Porter and has been sung by Frank Sinatra, Bing Crosby, Lana Del Rey and Ella Fitzgerald among others.

Other English language songs about the French capital include "A Country Girl In Paris" by John Denver, "A Rainy Night In Paris" by Chris De Burgh, "An American In Paris" by George Gershwin, "April in Paris" by Louis Armstrong, "Going To Paris" by The Waterboys and "I Never Got Out Of Paris" by Sammy Davis Jr.

As for French language songs about the capital, Sous le Ciel de Paris by Yves Montand is definitely one to look out for. La Bohéme by Charles Aznavour is a fantastic song about a struggling artist living a bohemian life in Paris.

Les Amants de Paris by Edith Piaf and Madamoiselle de Paris by Jacqueline François are among the other many songs about Paris worth listening to.

Film

Paris is widely regarded as being the home of cinema, due to the fact that the Lumière brothers gave the world its first glimpse of the entertainment offered by moving pictures in this city.

Since then, the famous Parisian landmarks have lit up the big screen on many memorable occasions. The city has also attracted numerous famous actors to live here or to just spend time soaking up the pleasure of a few days in Paris.

Actors Who Have Lived Here

Juliette Binoche, Emma Watson, Jeanne Moreau, Marion Cottilard, Julie Delpy, Salma Hayek, Natalie Portman, Gerard Depardieu and Scarlett Johansson are among the famous actors and actresses to have called this fine city home.

Films Featuring Paris

The list of films partially or entirely set in Paris is as long and hugely varied as you would expect. From *The Hunchback of Notre Dame* to *Before Sunset* and from *French Kiss* to *Midnight in Paris*, this city has been seen by many directors as offering the perfect backdrop to their movies.

Among the latest big films set here are *The Pink Panther 2*, *Inception* and *Sherlock Holmes: A Game of Shadows*.

Of course, as well as the English language films there have also been numerous more French films made here. These include excellent movies like *L'Atalante*, *Les Enfants du Paradis* and *Paris, je t'aime*.

Paris - Top 10 Attractions

You know that a city is a world class tourist destination when whittling down the list of the main attractions to just 10 is an incredibly tough task.

Paris is visited annually by some 32 million tourists and each of them no doubt has a long list of the things that they absolutely can't afford to miss seeing. Among the sights that could be considered as unmissable are the following.

The Eiffel Tower

iv

Without doubt, the very first thing that many new visitors to Paris want to see is the Eiffel Tower. This iconic structure has captured the imagination of the world ever since it was erected for the 1889 Universal Exposition.

Roughly 7 million people visit the Tower every year, although many more view it, photograph it and feel in awe of it from a distance. It is especially pretty after dark, when it lights up and sparkles in the Parisian night.

It is possible to walk up all 704 steps or to take the lift up pretty much all, day long, with access until at least 11pm every night, although on summer nights it remains open until midnight. There are restaurants and shops on the way up and the views of Paris from the 2nd floor and upwards are just incredible.

Arc De Triomphe

v

This beautiful 50 metre tall monument sits at the end of the Champs Élysées and is only a relatively short distance from the Eiffel Tower and other big attractions. It was built to honour the soldiers who had fought in the Napoleonic Wars and French Revolutionary Wars

As well as the inscriptions and images on the arch, it is contains the Tomb of the Unknown Soldier. It was Napoleon who ordered it built in 1806 but the work too so long to complete that the emperor died 15 years before it was finished.

The Clueless Tourist's

The Arc de Triomphe sits in a roundabout at the centre of 12 avenues that radiate out from it, making it the ideal spot for the victory parades that have passed here over the years. This famous structure has seen Napoleon's body pass under it, as well as that of Victor Hugo. It was also the scene of the famous stunt when Charles Godefroy flew his plane through it.

Not all visitors realise that it is possible to climb up to the top of the arch. The first step is to avoid the busy traffic by going through one of the underpasses. Once there a lift can be taken to the attic museum. A further 46 steps can be walked up in order to get to the very top and see a fantastic view of Paris.

The Louvre

The massive Louvre Palace building houses the world's most visited museum. Among the 35,000 objects on display here are the Mona Lisa, the Venus De Milo, Liberty Leading the People, the Law Code of Hammurabi and the Great Sphinx of Tanis.

With miles and miles of exhibits in this giant building, there is no way to visit every single thing on display. Over 9 million people visit the Louvre every year and it seems safe to say that most of them attempt to see the Mona Lisa, which is in the part of the museum where crowds tend to be heaviest.

However, there is a lot more to this place than just Da Vinci's masterpiece. In fact, there are 8 different collections here, covering the likes of Egyptian, Greek, Roman and Islamic Art.

The Champs Élysées

vii

This wide and elegant boulevard is one of the main streets in Paris. It covers over a mile from Place de la Concorde to the Arc de Triomphe on Place Charles de Gaulle.

It is well known for containing a mixture of high quality shops, cafes and theatres, with the locals calling it the most beautiful avenue in the world. Big name stores on the Champs Élysées include Cartier, Benetton, Louis Vitton, Lacoste, Nike, Hugo Boss, Zara and Adidas.

The end of the Tour de France typically occurs here, while on Bastille Day (14 July) the biggest military parade in Europe passes down the avenue with the President looking on. It is also common for large scale celebrations and protests to take place here.

The Clueless Tourist's

Notre Dame de Paris

viii

One of the oldest and most instantly recognisable religious buildings in the world, the Notre Dame cathedral is a wonderful example of French Gothic architecture. The name Notre Dame de Paris translates as Our Lady of Paris and it is a timeless symbol of the city.

Among the most interesting features here are the famous gargoyles, the pretty stained glass, the interesting sculptures and the giant bell known as Emmanuel.

The cathedral sits near the Seine river and it is free to visit any day. It is also possible to climb up to the towers, although there are 380 steps to get up here and you need to pay a small fee for access. Around 13 million people visit here every year, making it the most visited site in the city.

The Clueless Tourist's

Sacré Cœur

ix

This eye-catching basilica sits on the raised area at Montmartre, which is the highest point in the city and is surrounded by an interesting neighbourhood.

Work began here in 1875 and it was completed by 1914. It is a dazzlingly white building, due to the fact that the stone used in its construction never gets dulled or dirtied by pollution or bad weather.

There is a pretty, peaceful garden here but the most spectacular part is probably the stunning view offered from the top of the dome. The church can be entered free of charge from 6 am until 10.30 each evening but the dome can only be accessed until 6pm or 7pm, depending upon the time of year.

Musée d'Orsay

The Clueless Tourist's

This magnificent museum is housed in an old railway station on the left bank of the Seine river. The contents are mainly from French artists from the period 1848 through to 1915 and include many intriguing masterpieces.

The collections here cover paintings as well as photographs, sculptures and furniture. Among the highlights is the world's biggest collection of impressionist and post-impressionist pieces. Painters who have their works on show include Gauguin, Monet, Van Gogh, Renoir and Cézanne.

The Musée d'Orsay was opened in 1986 and attracts some 3 million visitors each year.

The Centre Georges Pompidou

This giant complex covers a range of attractions that make it interesting for tourists. Among them is the Musée National d'Art Moderne. This is the biggest modern art museum in Europe and one of the most visited art museums anywhere on the planet.

There are more than 10,000 works of art in the Musée National d'Art Moderne but there also other things worth seeing in the Centre Georges Pompidou too. For example, the enormous public information library and IRCAM; which is a centre devoted to musical research.

Overall, the centre receives more than 5 million visitors per year, with more than half that number visiting the museum while they are there. The large sculpture outside of the centre is called Horizontal and stands some 25 feet tall.

Cité des Sciences et de l'Industrie

xi

Yet another fascinating place to visit in the French capital is the Cité des Sciences et de l'Industrie. This is Europe's biggest science museum and is visited by some 5 million people annually.

The location of this museum is in Parc de la Villette, which sits in the 19th arrondissement and is one of the city's biggest parks. The aim of this museum is to promote science and technical knowledge as widely as possible.

The Cité museum hosts an IMAX theatre, a planetarium and a submarine, as well as special kid's and teenager's zones.

Pére Lachaise Cemetery

xii

Not many cities have a cemetery among their list of top tourist attractions but few cities have a cemetery as beautiful and evocative as the Pére Lachaise Cemetery.

The Clueless Tourist's

It is said to be the most visited graveyard in the world, with around 2 million people believed to come here every year to pay their respects to the many famous residents who found there final resting place in this peaceful spot in Paris.

Among the famous people buried here are Oscar Wilde, Chopin and Jim Morrison. There are also many French presidents, writers and philosophers buried here.

Recommended Itineraries

There is so much to see and do in Paris that working out a sensible itinerary to cover it all can be tough. The fact that many visitors come here for short breaks means that it is even more important to make good use of the time spent in this historic city.

Day 1 – Notre Dame, a River Cruise and the Eiffel Tower

Many of the top sights in Paris lie alongside the Seine. Travelling along this river on a short cruise is a fine way to understand the basic layout of the city and to see some of the main attractions from an interesting point of view.

The shortest river trips will take you just an hour or so. Otherwise, a lunch or dinner cruise will typically run for up to 5 hours. A great idea is to visit the Notre Dame cathedral before a taking mid-day cruise with lunch. If time is short then you might need to take the Metro to the cruise departure point, typically close the Eiffel Tower. Otherwise, an invigorating walk along the river needn't take you too long. The distance from the cathedral to the tower is just under 3 miles and following the river makes it an easy route.

As mentioned, many of the cruises leave and arrive near the Eiffel Tower, meaning that a trip to this fabulous monument is a perfect way to carry on sight-seeing after reaching dry land again. Many tourists spend a fair bit of time just looking at the tower but you will need at least an hour or so if you plan to head up there.

If you have the time then you can enjoy dinner in one of the restaurants up here and watch the sun set over Paris. Once you get back down again you can enjoy the sight of the Eiffel Tower lit up in the Parisian evening. After this, a stroll along the Seine or to a different vantage point is a glorious way to end a day here.

If you take it easy then these three activities can fill up the best part of a memorable day. If you prefer to get around more quickly or are on a tight timescale it is definitely possible to fit in more as well.

Day 2- Arc de Triomphe, Champs Élysées and Tuileries Gardens

The Champs Élysées is a fantastic street for passing the best part of the day if you love shopping. It runs for a little over as mile and is lined with top class shops and restaurants.

You could easily pass a few hours strolling along this broad avenue and soaking up the delightful atmosphere in between stores. The presence of so many cafes and restaurants also means that it is a place where it is easy to stop for something to eat and drink along the way.

At either end of this avenue are two of the city's other great attractions; the Arc de Triomphe and the Tuileries Gardens. Each of these places is well worth at least an hour and possibly a lot more time if visited in a relaxed way. You can also take in the nearby, historic Place de la Concorde too.

Day 3- Louvre and Sacré Cœur

The massive size of the Louvre museum and the lengthy queues that form here mean that it isn't the sort of place where a flying visiting is recommended. Buying tickets in advance is a great idea but even so, a serious art or history fan could easily spend all day in here.

The Clueless Tourist's

While some tourists only make their way to the most popular exhibits, but it seems a real shame to miss out on the wealth of other items on display here.

A nice tip here is to visit on a Wednesday or Friday. On these days the closing time is extended from 6pm to 9.45pm. The doors open at 9am and long queues tend to form at the pyramid entrance by this time. The underground entrance at Carousel du Louvre usually has smaller queues.

Many tourists complain about the price of food in the Louvre, so you might prefer to wait and eat once you get outside again.

If the visit to the Louvre doesn't leave a huge amount of time for other things then the best option may be to simply head out to the Sacré Cœur basilica to end the day with a tremendous view of Paris.

It is a fairly long walk of close to 3 miles and you might need a map if you intend to try it this way. Paris is a very walkable city, though, and you are sure to see some great sights if you do this. On the other hand, the Metro will take you there very quickly and simply.

Day 4 - Cité des Sciences et de l'Industrie, Pére Lachaise Cemetry and Musée d'Orsay

Cramming these three top attractions into one day makes for a packed but hugely enjoyable day. The Cité des Sciences et de l'Industrie is a little way out from the centre, as it is located in the 19th arrondissement. It is a great place to spend a full morning before moving on elsewhere.

Paris is easy to get around by public transport, so getting out to the Pére Lachaise Cemetery after this should be easy. There are a few different options for getting here. If you are most interested in seeing Oscar Wilde's grave then the Gambetta station on line 3 is ideal. It is also worth getting a map, due to the size of the cemetery.

Finally, the Musée d'Orsay is open until late on Thursdays until 9.45pm. It closes at 6pm on other days, which may be too early for anyone who spent a long time in the other attractions on this itinerary.

Where to Eat

xiii

Paris has such a fabulous culinary heritage that eating out is one of the top attractions for many people visiting the French capital.

The choice of places to eat here is massive and almost unbelievably varied. Classy restaurants, humble street kiosks and just about everything else in between are to be found in the city, with French cuisine and international fare often sitting side by side on the same streets. So, where are the best places to eat here?

Le Petit Vendôme

The colourful and informal eatery has a great location on the Rue des Capucines near the Rue de la Paix and provides what feels like a typical Parisian restaurant experience. It tends to get very crowded here, so if you don't like eating shoulder to shoulder with other diners then you might be put off by the crowds.

Otherwise, tasty sandwiches and baguettes are the order of the day here, although full, hearty meals are also available. The prices are very reasonable and the use of fresh, local products is great to see. Another point in its favour for many tourists is that it is incredibly popular with locals, probably more so than with tourists.

Le Jourdain

This is a classy but reasonably inexpensive restaurant on the Rue des Couronnes, in the Belleville neighbourhood. Seafood is the speciality here and the wines also come highly recommended.

The service in Le Jourdain is something that many visitors go away raving about, as the waiters go out of their way to make all of the diners enjoy the experience. Fans of good seafood, good wine and a top class dining experience will enjoy it.

Le Cinq

This elegant and refined restaurant in the Four Seasons Hotel on the avenue George V blows away diners with some incredible meals.

With 2 Michelin stars to its name you can expect exquisite food and an impeccable level of service. It is far from being the cheapest place to eat in Paris but it is certainly a contender for being one of the very best.

Pirouette

With an enviable location near Les Halles in the 1st arrondissement, Pirouette is a great choice for anyone who doesn't want to stray too far from the heart of Paris for food. It has a clean, modern look and a varied menu that covers classic French cuisine with many unique touches.

The location and the quality of the food mean that it isn't a particularly cheap place to eat but, as with many restaurants in this city, the quality means that it is still great value for money.

Soul Kitchen

Paris isn't just about expensive, elegant places to eat. This city also has a great number of budget eateries with interesting menus and a great deal of atmosphere. Among them we find the funky Soul Kitchen, which sits near the steps of Montemartre.

It is a friendly place where coffee, pastries and good food can be enjoyed in a relaxed setting and for a decent price.

Le Jules Verne

The idea of dining part of the way up the Eiffel Tower is such a fabulous idea that the restaurant Le Jules Verne is an idea well worth considering. It is a fairly expensive place to eat but the views from its 2nd floor setting are pretty remarkable.

The food here has received good online reviews from diners but for many tourists it is the outstanding vistas that make this restaurant one of their favourite places to visit in Paris.

Saravana Bhavan

Paris is one of the world's best cities for luxury dining but it also has more than its fair share of budget eateries as well. One cheap place to eat that stands out is the Saravana Bhavan.

This is actually part of a chain that is present in about a dozen countries. They deal in vegetarian meals from the Southern part of India using fresh ingredients. This spotlessly clean 80 seater restaurant in the 10th arrondissement offers an interesting alternative to the more typical Parisian restaurants.

Le Sergent Recruteur

There are few places that offer such a range of gastronomic treats as the French capital. Those visitors who want to enjoy all of the sensory pleasure that Paris offers might want to check out the menu at the glorious Le Sergent Recruteur.

This certainly isn't a cheap place to dine but the innovative versions of French classics served here are well worth paying for. The food is served in a classy setting and with the kind of faultless waiting service you would expect from a restaurant as good as this.

Where to Stay

There are few cities anywhere on Earth with more hotels than Paris. The enduring popularity of the city of light among tourists means that there is a massive number of places to spend a night here.

With thousands of hotels and hostels to choose from, it all comes down to finding the right style and price for your situation. The first thing to consider is how central you want to be. Paris is generally regarded as a city where it pays to be as central as possible, as many of the top attractions will be within walking distance in this way.

However, the excellent Metro system here means that as long as you are close to a station you will be able to get around easily. Further out from the centre you can also expect to get better value for money in your hotel room.

Bearing all of that in mind, the following are some of the top choices to consider.

Mercure Paris Centre Tour Eiffel

If you want to be right in the thick of the action in Paris then this perfectly located hotel will suit you right down to the ground. As the name suggests, it is close to the Eiffel Tower, which means that it is also close to many other top landmarks.

There is a Metro station within walking distance too, meaning that getting out further from the centre is also easy. For a 4 star hotel in the centre of one of the world's greatest cities the prices are pretty reasonable.

Book here: http://www.mercure.com/gb/hotel-2175-mercure-paris-centre-eiffel-tower-hotel/index.shtml

Four Seasons Hotel George V

For a luxury break in an enviable location this Four Seasons hotel is hard to beat. This is a 5 star hotel and it is situated closed to the wonderful Champs Élysées.

Among the highlights are the fantastic Le Cinq restaurant, the spa and the friendly but discreet staff. A night here isn't cheap but it is an unforgettable experience in a quality hotel.

Book here: http://www.fourseasons.com/paris/

Hotel Da Vinci

For something a bit different this stunning boutique hotel in the St Germain des Près area is highly recommended. The rooms are all carefully decorated and unique. It is another pricey but memorable place to stay.

The location of this 4 star hotel is interesting, as it has a quiet local feel but is only a few minutes walking distance from the nearest Metro station and from attractions such as the Louvre.

Book here: http://www.hoteldavinciparis.com/en/

Absolute Budget

At the opposite end of the scale from the luxury hotels covered earlier, Absolute Budget is a no frills hostel with rock bottom prices. It is a relatively new place too, having only opened its doors in 2010.

There are both private rooms and dorms on offer here, with not a huge difference in price between them. The room are brighter and more cheerful than the low prices might suggest, though. This budget hostel is located close to a Metro station in the 11th arrondissement and is convenient for Pére Lachaise cemetery and other top sights.

Book here: http://www.absolute-paris.com/

Plug Inn Boutique Hostel

A great location in a quiet street in lovely Montmartre is the main reason for considering this budget accommodation choice. It used to be a plain and simple budget hotel but a smart makeover has turned it into an eye-catching boutique hostel.

It has private rooms with en-suite bathrooms as well as traditional shared dorms. It is only a few minutes walk from Moulin Rouge and about the same distance from the closest Metro stop.

Book here: http://plug-inn.fr/

Relais Christine

This lovely boutique hotel sits in the Saint-Germain des Prés neighbourhood and is only a short walk from Notre Dame. The modern rooms are all artistically decorated and offer modern services such as Wi-Fi and flat screen TVs.

Among the highlights are the pretty garden, the charming breakfast room and the lounge bar. There is also a well-stocked fitness centre here.

Book here: http://www.relais-christine.com/

Le Relais des Halles

The Le Relais des Halles is a stylish hotel in the centrally located Les Halles. It is close the Metro and has numerous restaurants and jazz clubs around it. Walking from here to some of the other main attractions in Paris is also easy enough.

This is a boutique hotel that offers modern facilities and a friendly service with some thoughtful touches.

Book here: http://hotel-relais-des-halles.com/en/index.html

Nightlife

In a cosmopolitan city with a population of 2 million and a metropolitan area of some 12 million it is clear that there are nightlife options here for just about every taste under the sun.

The city of Paris caters for all tastes with its impressive range of pubs, clubs and cafés, some of which are world famous and others well-kept secrets frequented by more locals than by tourists.

Jazz Club Etoile - Website: http://www.jazzclub-paris.com/en/

Jazz remains a hugely popular musical style in the French Capital, with lots of clubs having live music on at night. The Jazz Club Etoile is close to the Champs Élysées and many famous names have taken to the stage here over the years.

The club is based in the Méridien Etoile Hotel and has been on the go since the 1970s. There are plenty of options when it comes to whisky and cocktails to drink while listening to some quality live music.

Moulin Rouge – Website:
http://www.moulinrouge.fr/?lang=en

The infamous Moulin Rouge has been the site of dancing and decadence since it first opened its doors in 1889, although the original building was burned down long ago and replaced by a new one. It is still an obligatory stop for many tourists looking for an exciting night out and a timeless show.

The Moulin Rouge is in the 18th arrondissement and is close to the Blanche Metro station. It is easily spotted due to the iconic red windmill on the building. Tickets for a music and dance show can be booked online in advance and dinner can be eaten here too.

Frog and Princess – Website:
http://www.frogpubs.com/pub-princess-paris.php

There are numerous good pubs in Paris, with many located in the Latin Quarter. The Frog and Princess is a solid choice for a beer and a burger in a friendly setting. It focuses on American food and is a fine place to start a night out in Paris.

 It lies in the heart of Saint Germain and attracts a mixed crowd of young students, tourists and locals.

There is also a very decent selection of microbrewed beers to check out here.

Buddha Bar – Website: http://www.buddhabar.com/en/restaurant-bar-buddha-bar-paris-20

The zen ambience in this popular bar makes it ideal for a relaxing evening of drinking and enjoying some cool world music. It is located on the Champs Élysées and is open until 2am.

This bar has a good food menu and is the perfect choice if you want an achingly cool bar with a fantastic and unique vibe. It isn't cheap but it is a wonderful spot to chill out in.

Café Beaubourg – Website: http://cafebeaubourg.com/en/

The fabulous location across from the Centre Pompidou is the biggest attraction here. Simply put, this is a wonderful spot for people watching from the terrace.

It has a stark, modern design that isn't to everyone's taste but it is seen by many Parisians and tourists as the perfect place to meet in the evening. The menu is extensive and it has long opening hours, meaning that it is ideal for taking a break during a hectic day of sight-seeing.

Au Petit Suisse – Website: http://aupetitsuisse.fr/en

Another spot with a terrific location is the ever popular Au Petit Suisse. It overlooks the Jardin du Luxembourg. This café has been going strong since the end of the 18 century and has a homely feel to it.

It is small and has a little terrace and mezzanine level. Lunch is served but for many people it is simply an ideal spot for unwinding with a glass of wine a little later in the day.

Museums/Art Galleries

xiv

Paris is regarded by many as being the best city in the world for culture vultures keen to see as many valuable pieces of art and historic treasures as they can.

No trip to the French capital is complete without a visit to at least one museum or art gallery. Each of them has their own speciality, meaning that there are different reasons for visiting each of them.

The Louvre

If you want to see some of the world's finest pieces of art in an unforgettable setting the Louvre is a fine choice. It does get astonishingly busy, though. Those visitors who are only in Paris for a few days may worry about losing too much of their valuable sight-seeing time in the queues here.

Once you are inside the Louvre there is just so much to marvel at that is easy to get caught up in the excitement and spend hours wandering around. Ideally, a keen art fan will come here with a clear idea of what they want to see and where to find it. The fact that this giant museum is so well located means that it is possible to fit a visit into most itineraries in central Paris.

Musée d'Orsay

While the Louvre has a stunningly vast collection of items covering wildly different places and time periods, the Musée d'Orsay is more tightly focussed on relatively modern French art from the 19th and 20th centuries, with some notable exceptions.

The setting in an old railway station is unique and there is no shortage of wonderful exhibits on show. However, the smaller scale smaller crowds mean that it is usually slightly easier to fit it into a short visit than is the case with the Louvre. Location-wise, there is no need to travel too far from the centre to enjoy the art here.

Musée National d'Art Moderne

Visitors to Paris with a more modern taste in art will be delighted at the massive selection on show at the Musée National d'Art Moderne, located in the Centre Georges Pompidou. There is a lot to get around here and the wealth of other attractions in the neighbourhood means that setting aside a full day for the visit is a good idea.

It is an easy museum to visit, with a bright and airy feel. As with the other top cultural attractions in Paris it can get exceedingly busy, though.

Shopping

Many people spend years dreaming of going on a glamorous shopping trip to Paris. The French capital is rightly famous for its fashion, perfume, art and so much more.

The good news is that this city isn't just about expensive goods and luxury shopping experiences. There is also enough variety in the stores and markets here to keep budget-conscious shoppers happy too.

Champs Élysées

This wide and impeccably elegant boulevard is the first place that most people think of when they imagine what it would be like to go shopping in Paris. This has traditionally been an expensive and very up-market street on which to go shopping.

These days, it is perhaps a little bit more accessible for more shoppers, as some big retail chains have moved in. There has been local resistance to this change, but there is no doubt that it has now opened up the Champs Élysées to a wider range of shoppers.

Galeries Lafayette

This classic Paris shopping destination has an elegant feel to it. The main location is a giant department store on the Boulevard Haussmann, which is in the 9th arrondissement, although it also has other locations now as well.

This main store has a beautiful dome at its centre and offers popular fashion shows each week. Galeries Lafayette is considered as being an icon of French fashion and lifestyle. Also to be found on the same road is the equally impressive Printemps store.

Flea Markets

Some visitors to the French capital prefer the joy of rummaging about in the city's flea markets while looking for bargain purchases. For example, the massive market at Marché aux Puces de St-Ouen sprawls over 7 hectares in the north of Paris and is widely considered as being the biggest flea market in the world. Around 180,000 people are thought to come here each weekend.

Another popular Parisian flea market is the one at Les Puces de Montreuil. This is less touristy than the one at St-Ouen and is particularly good for finding interesting antiques at decent prices. Finally, the Marché aux Puces de la Porte de Vanves is another terrific flea market in Paris.

Faubourg Saint-Honoré

This central street in Paris is fantastic for designer fashion and ultra-trendy shops. It is not as visually attractive a street as the Champs Élysées but many people consider it to be the most important fashion street on the planet, due to the fact that just about every major fashion label has a presence here.

Yves Sant Laurent. Hermes, Versace, Lancome and Lanvin are some of the top names found here. As well as the household names, many of the trendiest labels in the Paris fashion scene are located here. It is also home to some of the city's principal embassies and Élysée Palace.

Le Marais

For a unique and utterly fascinating shopping trip, it is hard to beat the Le Marais quarter of Paris. This is a lively zone with a wide mixture of different types of store. From luxury fashion brands to vintage clothing and from high quality art and antiques to unique hand-crafted goods, the Le Marais area has a lot to check out. This is also one of the top spots in the French capital for food shopping.

This is an historic area in the centre of Paris which is spread out over the 3rd and 4th arrondissements. It has a wonderful old world feel that makes it ideal for tourists looking to stroll around cobbled alleys while doing some shopping.

Saint Germain des Prés

The hip St Germain district is a great place to check out some chic boutiques and to browse in quality book stores. Retro clothing is also big here, while the Bon Marché is a classic department store in in this area.

This is also possibly the best place to buy art in Paris, as it contains dozens of galleries with art of all types.

Les Halles

Les Halles has a strong tradition as being an important focal point of shopping expeditions, first as a giant outdoor food market and then as a shopping zone. The underground mall called Le Forum des Halles is filled with global chain stores, while the Rue de Rivoli also has many big name stores too.

As you move towards the Louvre end of Les Halles the big chains are gradually replaced by independent stores selling antiques, arts and crafts.

Parks/Activities

xvi

Paris is a wonderful city for spending some time outdoors in one of the many parks dotted around here. There are many to choose from, with a wide range of activities on offer in the best of them.

Bois de Boulogne

This massive park is located in the 16 arrondissement and is the second biggest park in the city of Paris. It covers 845 hectares, within which are a number of lakes, a zoo, an amusement park, botanical gardens and many other features.

The park contains a series of greenhouses known the Jardin des Serres d'Auteuil, which contains thousands of plants. In terms of sports, there are two hippodromes for horse racing and the tennis stadium where the French Open is held annually.

The Boise de Boulogne is a popular spot at weekends for picnics, jogging, pony rides and cycling. It is also common to see people use remote control boats on the water. A three day long party and music festival is held here in July.

Bois de Vincennes

This is the biggest public park in Paris, covering some 995 hectares and taking up about a tenth of whole area of the city. It is located in the western part of Paris and has a zoo, 4 lakes, a botanical garden, a horse racing track and a velodrome.

The Bois de Vincennes is in the 12th arrondissement and is filled with flowers, trees and grassy areas. The Jardin Tropical de Paris covers 4 and a half hectares of the park and is filled with exotic plants from all round the French empire.

The Ferme Georges-V is a small scale farm that children can visit, to see the pigs, sheep and crops. It is a popular park with families and simply strolling around it is a pleasurable experience.

Luxembourg Gardens

Located in the 6th arrondissement, the Jardin du Luxembourg is a pretty park that is spread over 23 hectares. The cultivated lawns, flower beds and tree-filled avenues make it a delightful place to stroll around. Highlights included the lovely Medici fountain, the statues of French royalty and the model sailboats.

These gardens have been around since the early 17th century. It is a peaceful and relaxing atmosphere that makes it ideal for families and couples. Indeed, there is a secure playground with a vintage carousel and a puppet theatre here.

Tuileries Garden

The famous Tuileries Garden is centrally located in the 1st arrondissement, between the Louvre and the Place de la Concorde. It was created in the 16th century and is seen as a place for locals to meet, to celebrate, to parade and to take it easy.

The Arc de Triomphe du Carrousel is one of the main features here, while the garden is also home to a number of fine statues. There is a raised terrace and a moat, while the open end at the East has the big square known as the Grand Carré.

To the west is the Orangerie Museum (Musée de l'Orangerie) and the Jeu de Paume (Galerie nationale du Jeu de Paume).

Parc de Bercy

This public park sits in the 12th arrondissement, by the banks of the Seine. It runs to almost 14 hectares and is made up of three different gardens which are connected by foot bridges. The National Library of France is located on the opposite side of the river.

The Romantic Gardens section is best known for its dune and fish ponds. The Flowerbeds is all about different types of plants, while The Meadows is an open space with many trees shading the lawns.

The Musée des Arts Forains (private funfair related museum) and the Cinémathèque Française (film museum with daily screenings of films) are among the buildings in this park.

Parc Monceau

This is an attractive outdoor space in the 8th arrondissement of Paris. It is over 8 hectares in size and was designed as an English garden with a Chinese influence. It is famous for its different follies, many of which are cleverly designed reconstructions of diverse buildings from around the world. Among these are an Egyptian pyramid, a Dutch windmill and a Chinese fort.

Statues are dotted about the park in a seemingly random way, while there are play areas for kids. It is also popular with people wanting to get hooked up to the internet, as it offers free Wi-Fi access.

Parc Floral de Paris

This public park in the 12th arrondissement is also a botanical garden. It has been around since 1969 and is home of flower shows throughout the year. Stretching to 31 hectares, it is among the largest park in the city and contains a large number of interesting features.

The Parc Floral de Paris has a concert stage, exhibition halls, a restaurant, a children's playground, a miniature railway and an art gallery. Flower gardens can be found throughout the park, with many of these focusing on one flower or else culinary herbs or medicinal plants.

Neighbourhoods

Part of the immense charm of Paris comes from the fact that it is made up of so many different neighbourhoods, each with their own charms and unique appeal.

To get the most out of this vast and diverse city it is important to understand what each of the different neighbourhoods offer to the visitor.

Latin Quarter

The Quartier Latin is a wonderfully atmospheric neighbourhood that runs across the 5th and 6th arrondissements. It is famous for its bohemian background, for being home to many students and for housing a number of the French capital's most beautiful tourist attractions.

The Latin Quarter is filled with historic winding streets, book shops, music shops and welcoming cafes. It is also a popular for its bars and nightlife scene. The food offering is varied, with many ethnic restaurants rubbing shoulders with typical bakeries in this neighbourhood.

This is a trendy neighbourhood that is also within walking distance of attractions such as Notre Dame and other central parts of the city. The Pantheon is one of the most recognisable parts of the Latin Quarter and is used by many locals and tourists as a meeting place. La Sorbonne is an historic university in this neighbourhood, while the Sunday market on Rue Mouffetard is a great spot for doing some shopping and people-watching.

Champs Élysées

It is easy to think of the Champs Élysées neighbourhood as being just the wide and attractive boulevard that bears this name. However, there is a lot more to it than that. From the Arc de Triomphe at one end to the Place de la Concorde at the other, this is a wonderful zone that encapsulates many of the things that Paris is famous for.

It is a high class area, with exclusive boutiques, expensive houses and classy restaurants. There are many things to do in this part of Paris that attract tourists to the Champs Élysées. Theatres, cinemas and museums are all to be found here.

For many visitors this neighbourhood is the epitome of the romantic, charming city that they were looking for in Paris. It would be easy to spend an entire break in the capital in this just one neighbourhood, as it has more style, beauty and interesting things to do than just about anywhere else in the world.

Bastille

Bastille is the Parisian neighbourhood where the bustle of modern day France collides with old world charm, resulting in an enchanting zone with stunning results. This is the place where gorgeous, historic streets are lined with pretty shops and lively bars. It is also where the nightlife is loud and hugely enjoyable.

The July Column is a great focal point here, as it stands proudly in the Place de la Bastille and acts as a reference point for travellers. The broad avenues in this area are fantastic but it is by wandering the narrow side streets that a tourist can really get a feel for life in this historically important neighbourhood.

The Bastille Opera House is the home of the Paris Opera. Meanwhile, the presence of the Seine gives travellers the chance to stroll alongside the water while sampling a variety of food stalls and amusement parks.

Montmartre

The lively Montmartre district feels almost like a village within the city of Paris. Its busy streets in the 18th arrondissement are typically filled with both locals and tourists alike. To many, this feels more like the real, authentic Paris than any other part of the city.

Montmartre contains the highest point in the French capital meaning that it is an ideal area for seeing a stunning panoramic view of Paris. The stunning Sacré Cœur basilica sits at the top of the hill and offers the perfect place to survey the city from.

The steep streets leading up to the Sacré Cœur are lined with souvenir stalls, restaurants, cafes and shops. It is an area that encourages visitors to explore it on foot and to slowly unravel the timeless charms of an authentic Parisian neighbourhood.

Le Marais

This is a delightful central part of Paris, where the old world beauty of the amazing Place des Vosges rubs shoulders with excellent cuisine, a strong Jewish heritage, cultural attractions and lots of art.

This neighbourhood is sometimes called by the name of Old Paris and it is easy to see why. The timeless elegance of Le Marais brings to mind a different century, while it also offers easy access to modern treats.

Winding cobbled streets lead the inquisitive traveller to beautiful old buildings, art galleries, bars, street food kiosks and a lot more. The lively feel to the night-time scene makes it a popular destination after dark. Gay and lesbian places are more plentiful here than in other parts of the city, but there is something here for everyone to enjoy.

While there are some classy French gourmet restaurants in this part of Paris, it is also a fine spot to try out some ethnic street food in a unique and memorable setting.

République

République is a fascinating Parisian area that spills over into the 3rd, 10th and 11th arrondissements. The Place de la République lies at the heart of the zone but there is a lot more to it than that.

With excellent transport links to the rest of the city and a cool, hip feel, this is a fabulous base for a stay in the French capital. République has a strong artistic and musical scene, while the food served here is as cosmopolitan as it is tempting.

There are many traditional local shops here, such as butchers and bakeries. The trendy Rue Oberkampf is a great place to head for some food and drinks. The Centre Pompidou, the food market on Rue de Bretagne and the numerous art galleries all vie for attention in this great neighbourhood.

Louvre – Tuileries

There can be few neighbourhoods anywhere on the planet that pack in as much art, tradition and history at this beautiful zone at the heart of Paris. A walk through Louvre – Tuileries turns into an incredible journey of discovery, as the traveller passes from one marvel to another.

Home to the gorgeous Tuileries Gardens and the incredible Louvre museum, this is a neighbourhood that most tourists spend a fair amount of time in. Away from those massive attractions, this is also a zone where shopping and eating can be carried out in an elegant, refined setting.

Its location alongside the Seine leads to some unbelievable photo opportunities and lovely evening strolls. For those who are still keen to soak up more culture the museums called Le Jeu de Paume and l'Orangerie are both well worth a visit.

Notre Dame – Ile de la Cité

This is the part of Paris that many people instantly picture when they think about this city. Of course, the iconic Notre Dame church is somewhere not to be missed on any visit the French capital.

Part of this neighbourhood sits on an island in the middle of the Seine, with the iconic Notre Dame church the main focal point for most tourists. However, those who wander off the beaten track away from the implacable gaze of the famous gargoyles will discover parks, gardens and interesting stores here too.

In a city as vast and fascinating as Paris it is difficult to call any one neighbourhood the highlight. Having said that, no visit to the city should miss out on the pleasures offered by Notre Dame – Ile de la Cité.

After exploring here there are numerous public transport options for getting out to see the rest of the capital. In addition, a stroll across the lovely old bridge to the Latin Quarter is a great option for those who want to walk around some more.

Conclusion

xvii

A trip to Paris is a dream come true for lots of people, just as it has been for so many adventurous travellers throughout the centuries.

The unique blend of art, fashion, culture and cuisine to be found here makes it the kind of destination that everyone can enjoy in their own way. From gazing up at the Eiffel Tower to wandering round the Louvre and from shopping in a massive flea market to enjoying a picnic in the park, this is a city that everyone falls in love with in different ways.

Paris Travel Guide

The excellent public transport system, the proximity of many attractions and the attractiveness of Paris as a walkable city means that getting around and seeing numerous world famous attractions is possible even in a short time frame. However, to get this right it is necessary to understand where to see and what to do.

Due to the size and diversity of this city it is well worth taking some time to research the different attractions and districts. In this way, it is possible to make the most of the time spent here and not miss out on any of the wonders that Paris offers.

The Clueless Tourist's

Image acknowledgements

80

23529486R00051

Printed in Poland
by Amazon Fulfillment
Poland Sp. z o.o., Wrocław